ALICIA IN WONDER TIERRA
(or I Can't Eat Goat Head)

A Play in Two Acts
by
SILVIA GONZALEZ S.

Loosely based on Lewis Carroll's
"Alice in Wonderland"
(with a touch of "The Wizard of Oz")

Dramatic Publishing
Woodstock, Illinois • London, England • Melbourne, Australia

*** NOTICE ***

The amateur and stock acting rights to this work are controlled exclusively by THE DRAMATIC PUBLISHING COMPANY without whose permission in writing no performance of it may be given. Royalty fees are given in our current catalogue and are subject to change without notice. Royalty must be paid every time a play is performed whether or not it is presented for profit and whether or not admission is charged. A play is performed any time it is acted before an audience. All inquiries concerning amateur and stock rights should be addressed to:

DRAMATIC PUBLISHING
P. O. Box 129, Woodstock, Illinois 60098.

COPYRIGHT LAW GIVES THE AUTHOR OR THE AUTHOR'S AGENT THE EXCLUSIVE RIGHT TO MAKE COPIES. This law provides authors with a fair return for their creative efforts. Authors earn their living from the royalties they receive from book sales and from the performance of their work. Conscientious observance of copyright law is not only ethical, it encourages authors to continue their creative work. This work is fully protected by copyright. No alterations, deletions or substitutions may be made in the work without the prior written consent of the publisher. No part of this work may be reproduced or transmitted in any form or by any means, electronic or mechanical, including photocopy, recording, videotape, film, or any information storage and retrieval system, without permission in writing from the publisher. It may not be performed either by professionals or amateurs without payment of royalty. All rights, including but not limited to the professional, motion picture, radio, television, videotape, foreign language, tabloid, recitation, lecturing, publication, and reading are reserved. *On all programs this notice should appear:*

"Produced by special arrangement with
THE DRAMATIC PUBLISHING COMPANY of Woodstock, Illinois"

©MCMXCVI by
SILVIA GONZALEZ S.

Printed in the United States of America
All Rights Reserved
(ALICIA IN WONDER TIERRA
[or I Can't Eat Goat Head])

Cover design by Susan Carle

ISBN 0-87129-582-2

SYNOPSIS

Alicia enters a Mexican curio shop with her mother. Fascinated by the Latin American imports, Alicia reaches for a Mexican doll on display, but trips over Mexican pottery. The doll, Rosa, spins out of her hand and becomes a full size woman. She then disappears under a Mexican blanket. Alicia follows her and meets a variety of characters: A Day of the Dead sugar skull, an armadillo, and gang-bangers with faces painted to resemble Elvira wielding chicken claws. If touched by their chicken claw, the soul gets trapped in Mexican pottery. With the aid of a puppet, El Musico Tocando la Trumpeta (Ramon), Alicia heads to the Aztec Temple to find the Pottery Maker, and the truth about the trapped souls. During the journey, Alicia enlarges or shrinks by blowing into a trumpet, or breaking a piñata and meets a goat head steaming in an oven, a sad horny toad that is so ugly bricks keep falling on him, and the Tree of Heads. The tree holds the head of Pancho Villa, Charo, a mambo king, a pachuco, and a Hispanic Yuppie. Alicia also enters the Distorted Memory Forest, the Village of Laughter, and a maze of black velvet paintings. When she reaches the temple, she has menudo with the Aztec priest and his unique guests. Finally, Alicia finds the Pottery Maker and he tells her the truth about Mexican pottery. Rosa has been captured by the Elvira gang and it is up to Alicia to rescue her. Grateful to be saved, Rosa helps Alicia to go home. Alicia puts the Mexican blanket over her and finds herself back at the curio shop. Apparently, when she tripped over the pottery, she hit her head and knocked herself out. Before leaving the Mexican curio shop, Alicia's mother tells her that they must hurry home to help cook goat head for el compadre's dinner.

ALICIA IN WONDER TIERRA was produced at The Coterie Theatre as part of the Lila Wallace-Reader's Digest New Works for Young Audiences Program, October 10-November 5, 1995 in Kansas City, Missouri, with Jeff Church as Producing Artistic Director and Joette Pelster as Executive Director.

The Company

Marlene Mujica	Alicia
Richard Augustine	Storekeeper, Ramon
Linda Amayo	Sugar Skull, Armadilla, Hispanic Yuppie Head
Erika G. Gallcia	Elvira, Box With Legs, Flamenco Dancer, Villager, Echo
Philip blue owl Hooser	Horny Toad, Pachuco Head, Aztec Priest, Pottery Maker
Rosa Noyola de Reyes	Mother, Rosa Doll, Goat Head, Charo Head
Jerel Taylor	Cactus Man, Elvira, Soul, Mambo King, Villager, Echo, Chicken, Bull
Chato Villalobos	Dad, Elvira, Soul, Ventriloquist, Rosarita, Pancho Villa

Artistic and Production Company

José Cruz González	Director
Howard C. Jones	Set Design
Lynda K. Myers	Costume Design
Art Kent	Lighting Design
Greg Mackender	Sound Design
Ron Megee	Properties Master
Wendy Barsotti	Scenic Artist
Brad Shaw	Technical Director
Melanie Huntington	Stage Manager
Jennifer C. McCartney	Assistant Stage Manager

ALICIA IN WONDER TIERRA
(or I Can't Eat Goat Head)

A Play in Two Acts
For 8 or more actors, doubling

CHARACTERS

ALICIA
ROSA, the Mexican doll / MOM
RAMON, the puppet / STOREKEEPER
ARMADILLA
HORNY TOAD

OTHER CHARACTERS

Goat Head / Sugar Skull
Abuela / A Walking Box / Dad
Aztec priest / Mexican Man-Pottery Maker
Tree of Heads (Mambo King, Charo, Pancho Villa,
a *pachuco*, and a Hispanic Yuppie)
Elvira Gang #1-4 / Pottery Souls #1-4
Mexican Villagers #1-3 / Flamenco Dancer / Echo #1-3
Ventriloquist and Dummy Rosarita Refried
Cactus Man

*Cast number suggestion: at least eight actors
**Doubling, tripling or quadrupling can occur with Other Characters

ACT ONE

SCENE ONE

AT RISE: *ALICIA, whining like a teenage "Valley girl," follows her mother into a store full of Mexican curios.*

ALICIA. You said shopping.
MOM. This is shopping, *mija.*
ALICIA. The mall, Mom.
MOM *(picks up a decorative sugar skull).* ¿*A cuanto me lo dejas?*
STOREKEEPER. *Cuarenta.*
MOM. Very expensive.
STOREKEEPER. It should be. Someone made it with their bare hands.
ALICIA. Let's go.
STOREKEEPER. Look around, young lady. Your mother has a lot of money, and I want her to leave it here.
MOM. I don't have a lot of money.
STOREKEEPER. *No togues.*
MOM. Don't touch, *mija.*
ALICIA. He told me to look around.
STOREKEEPER. Look with your eyes, not with your fingerprints.
ALICIA *(looking at a price tag).* Ki-hoo-a-hoo-a.
MOM. What are you reading?
ALICIA. It says, Ki-hoo-a-hoo-a on this tag.
MOM. That's *Chihuahua.*

7

STOREKEEPER. No touching! You can touch in the back room, but only this once. Stay there long enough so your mother will buy something.

MOM. *Voy a comprar algo.*

STOREKEEPER. The last time you didn't buy one thing.

MOM. I miss these things.

STOREKEEPER. Then buy them and take them home. I need to pay my bills.

ALICIA. Mom. When we're done, can we go to the mall?

MOM. What a shame.

STOREKEEPER *(overlap on "shame")*. *Que lastima.*

MOM. Blame it on me. She wants clothes.

STOREKEEPER. I have beautiful clothes in the back. Go there and see if you like anything. *Andale.*

ALICIA. What else is back there?

STOREKEEPER. *Magia...(She doesn't understand.)* Magic.

MOM. She won't learn Spanish either.

STOREKEEPER. *Aye, caramba. (ALICIA wanders into another room—a world of more colorful items. She gazes at everything. She picks up a beautifully carved wooden horny toad. She touches the items even though the Spanish/English sign reads:* MIRAME Y NO TOQUES/LOOK BUT DON'T TOUCH. *ALICIA goes towards a display shelf with a variety of dolls.)*

ALICIA. Aztec instruments. A few flamenco combs. Here are Mexican dolls. It looks like a village on this counter. Useless stuff. What's this? *(She stares at one particular Mexican doll and takes it. It has long braids and large eyelashes. The lips are ruby red. The dress is filled with sequins.)* She's so pretty and it says "Rosa" under her shoe. Your name must be Rosa, then. You're pretty, but I don't want you.

MOM *(off)*. Are you causing trouble back there?

Act I   (or I Can't Eat Goat Head)   Page 9

(ALICIA steps back and accidentally trips over pottery. She falls behind the counter as the Mexican doll, Rosa, spins out of her hand. There's a BLACKOUT during the crash. When the lights return, ROSA is now a full size woman.)

ROSA. In the far reaches of the mind, I see you. I see myself. I see the whole world, and I wonder about so many things as I look out in a glaze. *(ROSA walks around and returns to the same spot.)* There is a hand that reaches to me. It wants me to take it. When I do, I see myself. *(ROSA walks around the room looking at the* piñatas.*)* I see your world, and I see my own. In both places I find isolation. I find loneliness. I find a person that I am and am not. I find a world made of animals in human clothing and humans in animal drapes. It hangs on a thread. *(ROSA runs to the stack of Mexican blankets, then throws a blanket over herself and disappears.)*

ALICIA *(coming out from behind the counter).* Wait!

(ALICIA runs to the blankets. A SUGAR SKULL floats up from the table and scares her. ALICIA throws the Mexican blanket over herself and disappears, too. Lights shift. A new place. Fog enters. ALICIA rises from it.)

ALICIA. Where am I?

(In the distance she sees ROSA running away. She tries to go after her, but the fog is overwhelming. Suddenly the SUGAR SKULL appears before her. It is floating and large, but friendly.)

SUGAR SKULL. *¿A donde vas?* Don't be afraid.
ALICIA. You are a skull.

SUGAR SKULL. Made of sugar. I'm not real. I represent the Day of the Dead. I could be a gift to someone. How much money do you have?

ALICIA. I have none.

SUGAR SKULL. NONE? Then I am wasting my time.

ALICIA. You are made of sugar?

SUGAR SKULL. Very sweet sugar.

ALICIA. Sugar *is* sweet.

SUGAR SKULL. Some sugar can be stale. Haven't you ever received a sugar skull from anyone?

ALICIA. No. Never.

SUGAR SKULL *(exaggerated inhale)*. That's shocking.

ALICIA. I think my parents may have gotten one when they were young, but I never have.

SUGAR SKULL *(exaggerated inhale)*. Never?

ALICIA. Never.

SUGAR SKULL. Never? Such things! This is a tradition here in Mexico.

ALICIA. We're not in Mexico. We're in a bazaar. There's a street out there in the middle of a city. This place is made up to look like "Little Mexico." Outside is a city.

SUGAR SKULL. NO!

ALICIA. Yes. I came in with my mom to buy a gift. I saw all these things that looked strange even though they looked familiar.

SUGAR SKULL. We are in Fresnillo, Zacatecas! I'm on a shelf in Carrillo's store waiting for the Day of the Dead.

ALICIA. Not. You are in a curio store in the United States. You will be bought as a curiosity and passed around as a very strange, yet folk-tale-like, object.

SUGAR SKULL *(exaggerated inhale)*. I'm not an object! I have a function! A very important function. It is a tradi-

Act I (or I Can't Eat Goat Head) Page 11

tion. Bah. I'm so sorry you ever came into the store. *(Darkness. The SKULL disappears.)*

ALICIA. Wait! Come back! The room is dark! I can't find the light switch.

(The fog starts to enter again. ALICIA runs to the wall and finds a switch, and turns it on. ROSA is standing in the distance looking at herself in the hand mirror. ALICIA sees her and ROSA runs again and disappears. Then ROSA reappears in another spot and disappears again. An ARMADILLO is sitting on a stool. A bright light shines on the ARMADILLO's face.)

ARMADILLA *(Texas accent)*. The sun dances on my face. I know if I gaze at the faraway ball-of-fire it'll burn my eyes. But I can't help it. I like it. I like it a lot. It feels so good on me. I love the mystery of—

VOICE *(off, Spanish accent)*. Don't sit in the sun! It'll wrinkle your face.

ARMADILLA *(continuing Texas accent throughout)*. I don't care.

VOICE *(off)*. Don't look at the sun! You'll go blind!

ARMADILLA. I don't care if I go blind.

VOICE *(off)*. Don't smile!

ARMADILLA. Why not?

VOICE *(off)*. A young lady doesn't smile too wide. They'll think she's asking for it.

ARMADILLA. I am asking for it. *(A slap is heard, ARMADILLA reacts. She then goes back to facing the sun. She opens her eyes, and rubs them for a few moments. She looks at the sun again, and then looks away. Purple, green, pink dots of light start to float around her. The colorful lights swing to the direction she faces.)* Floating amoebas, within the spots of refracted corneal light images. My delightful friends. There you are. You always come when I need you. *(The lights dance before her. Some go on her.)*

VOICE *(off)*. Don't look at the sun!

ARMADILLA. But I love the colorful spots.

VOICE *(off)*. You'll put a hole in your eyes.

ARMADILLA. So...A bright blue light, now green. Now bright pink. Any color I want. I just think of it. And the demon amoebas appear in a hazy splotch. See their brown arms extend outward? Spots, amoebas, then more spots. The amoebas look like...amoebas! The kind you see on a slide with a microscope. Well, just a bit different. How else can you describe what very few people see?

ALICIA. They say it's from the amniotic fluid that got in the fetus' eyes when they opened in the womb. *(She can't believe she said that.)*

ARMADILLA. Really? That was interesting...Ah, you dance before my eyes when I'm in rage. You descend to my nose, and then lift again as I blink my eyes. You, the lights, that dance before my eyes when I need you. *(To ALICIA.)* Who are you?

ALICIA. Alicia. Who are you?

ARMADILLA. Did the spots go?

ALICIA. I think they did.

ARMADILLA. So you saw them, too. I thought I was the only one who saw them. People who are very depressed see those spots.

ALICIA. I'm not depressed.

ARMADILLA. People who are confused, see those spots.

ALICIA. I'm not confused.

ARMADILLA. Yes, you are. *(A light shines on ARMADILLA's face. She closes her eyes and faces it.)*

VOICE *(off)*. You'll burn your face!

Act I (or I Can't Eat Goat Head) Page 13

ARMADILLA. I don't care. You smell something?
ALICIA. No.
ARMADILLA. I do.
ALICIA. What is it?
ARMADILLA. The faint odor of mascara. It's the Elvira gang. Go home!

(Suddenly, a gang of ELVIRAS surround ARMADILLA. [Their faces are painted like Elvira, the Empress of the Night on TV, and their bodies are of gang-bangers.] They surround ALICIA.)

ELVIRA #1. Hey, check out the coconut!
ELVIRA #2. She's a wetback!
ELVIRA #3. She's a *gringa!*
ELVIRA #4. She's a Mexican-American!
ELVIRA #2. No. We say *Latina!*
ELVIRA #3. She's a Chicana!!
ELVIRA #4. She's a *pocha.**
ELVIRA #1. She's a *pocha.*
ALL ELVIRAS. She's a *pocha.* She's a *pocha.* She's a *pocha.*
ALICIA. What do you want from me?
ELVIRA #1. Are you going around calling yourself a Hispanic?
ELVIRA #2. We don't like that word.
ELVIRA #3. We don't like *Chicana* either.
ELVIRA #4. That term is over.
ALICIA. I don't say anything.
ELVIRA #1. She doesn't say anything. Hear that? Nothing.
ELVIRA #4. Then what are you doing in our part of town?
ALICIA. I'm looking for someone.

---
* *po-sha=neither Mexican nor American*

ELVIRA #2. Are *you* looking for me?
ELVIRA #3. Are you looking for *me?*
ELVIRA #1. No. She's looking for me. Am I right? Am I RIGHT? *(ELVIRA #1 takes a chicken claw out of her pocket. The rest follow suit. They surround ALICIA.)*
ELVIRA #2. Elvee one.
ELVIRA #1. What?
ELVIRA #2. You're stepping on my foot
ELVIRA #1. That's Elvira three.
ELVIRA #3. My feet are over here.
ELVIRA #4. Wait a minute. I thought I was Elvira three.
ELVIRA #1. No, you're Elvira four.
ELVIRA #2. Who cares which number you are. We're a gang and that's all that matters.
ELVIRA #1. Hey, it matters to me. I'm in charge.
ELVIRA #2. Oh, yeah?
ELVIRA #1. Yeah.
ELVIRA #2. Oh, yeah?
ELVIRA #1. Yeah.

(During the argument ROSA has placed four marionette puppets nearby: A ballerina, a borracho (drunk), a novia (bride) and a musico tocando la trumpeta (trumpet player). ALICIA manages to get away from the ELVIRA gang and sees the puppets on the floor. She grabs one of them by the strings and spins it above her head causing a strange musical sound.)

ELVIRA #2. That sound is making my mascara run!
ELVIRA #3. Mine, too! *(ALICIA finishes one more swing of the puppet over her head and throws it at the ELVIRAS. They exit screaming, leaving a trail of mascara.)*

ALL ELVIRAS. I'd watch out if I were you. *(ALICIA notices slight movement from the puppet she just threw. She walks up to it.)*

PUPPET/RAMON. Did you have to pick me to throw at them?

ALICIA. I'm sorry.

PUPPET. You nearly broke my back. Look! Untangle my strings, then. *Por el amor de Dios.* Couldn't you have chosen the ballerina instead? She would have handled the toss better! She's so agile. Then again, *el borracho* wouldn't have felt a thing. He's always drinking.

ALICIA. I picked up the first thing.

PUPPET. *Mira mi trompeta.* Is it broken?

ALICIA. I'm so sorry.

PUPPET. How about the bride?

ALICIA. The bride over there?

PUPPET. *Si.* If you would have tossed her towards them, she would have handled the blow better with her dress. It's very fluffy, like cotton. She would have bounced like a ball.

ALICIA. Her dress would have gotten dirty.

PUPPET. Yeah, right. Brides are always fussy about their gowns...*(He looks at the trail of mascara on the ground.)* Lucky for you my trumpet made that sound. It scared them off. I heard about that gang before. They took a claw to another girl once. And she turned into that. *(Motioning.)*

ALICIA. Into what?

PUPPET. That over there. Look. Here. Take me over there... Turned her into pottery.

ALICIA. Pottery?

PUPPET. *All* that get touched by the claw turn into pottery. That is why there are so many in the store. The soul is forever trapped inside. Each design on the pot is the special imprint of each soul. You're lucky you weren't turned into pottery. I would have felt so sorry for you.

ALICIA. What if the pottery gets broken?

PUPPET. I don't know. I don't know what happens. Maybe the souls are released. Maybe they enter a piñata or something else. The only way to find out about that is to find the pottery maker and ask. What am I going to do about *mi trompeta?* No one is going to want to buy me.

ALICIA. Do you know where we can find the pottery maker? Maybe he can fix your trumpet.

PUPPET. I've never seen him. Just heard about him.

ALICIA. How can we find him?

PUPPET. Let's ask at the temple.

ALICIA. What temple?

PUPPET. The temple. You never heard of the Aztec temple before? Where are you from? Where is your sense of history?

ALICIA. I was never taught. All right. I never studied it. But I know it existed.

PUPPET. EXISTS! You have a lot to learn. And I have a lot to show you. We'll go together.

ALICIA. Let's go.

PUPPET. Wait. You will have to blow in my trumpet.

ALICIA. Why?

PUPPET. So I can go with you. You don't know your way around here, and I could be of some help.

ALICIA. All right. Thank you.

PUPPET. *De nada.* And call me Ramon.

ALICIA. Here goes, Ramon. *(She blows.)* YAO! My head is spinning.

(After blowing into the trumpet ALICIA becomes faint and falls to the floor. Lights spin around and when ALICIA

wakes up, she is now the size of the puppet. [Suggestion to create the illusion that ALICIA has shrunk, a human should now replace the puppet. He holds his own strings for movement.])

ALICIA. What happened to me?

RAMON. *Te has puesto de mi tamaño.*

ALICIA. Excuse me?

RAMON. You're my size now. Let's go.

ALICIA. Where are we going?

RAMON. To the temple. Remember? Or did your brain shrink in size too? Look, this will be a long journey. Can you handle it?

ALICIA. Sure.

RAMON. Well, let's get going before you go back to size. Going back to your original size has to be done at the right time, or else.

ALICIA. Or else what?

RAMON. Well, I hate to tell you.

ALICIA. Tell me, Ramon.

RAMON. Well, if we are going through a pipe, and you start to grow back, I can't be responsible for your *compression.*

ALICIA. Yikes! Would I ever get larger?!

RAMON. Only the Aztec temple has the answers. Hurry before the Elvira gang comes back with fresh mascara. *(They both exit.)*

SCENE TWO

AT RISE: *A brown BOX with legs enters. It stops, looks around then exits. ALICIA enters with RAMON.*

ALICIA. This is strange. I'm suddenly thinking about my grandmother. Did I ever tell you about her?

RAMON. No, we just started to get to know each other.

ALICIA. One day my brother and I discovered a horny toad basking in the sun. We argued over which one would take this great horny toad to school. The horny toad was about this big, and had these little horns coming out of—all parts of its body. My brother yelled, "Horny-TOE. Horny-TOE." Well, we both called it a TOE, t-o-e, rather than a TOAD, t-o-a-d. Our English wasn't that good then. Sounded the same to us. We were gazing at the oddity of this creature that was so interesting, and strangely exciting to us. We were both thinking of the instant fame we would get when we took it to school. "I'll take it to school!" said my brother. "No, I will!" I shouted back. "But I found it!" "I went up to it first." "But I—" and then—SQUISH—a brick smashed it, to death. The guts poured out of the mouth. "*El Diablo*" my grandmother said as she beckoned us to move away. She had the fear and pride of a grandmother protecting her grandchildren successfully from the devil...

RAMON. She killed it?

ALICIA. My brother and I just looked at each other...We got up and said absolutely nothing. No one was going to take it to school now. I thought about it, though...Naah. I changed my mind.

RAMON. I'm glad you did.

ALICIA. I was only seven.

RAMON. Such a story. Why did you tell me this?

ALICIA. I'm feeling funny. Now I'm suddenly being reminded of something else. Look, an oven. There in the dark.

(She walks to an oven and opens it. A GOAT HEAD is steaming in the oven.)

GOAT HEAD. *¡Hola! ¡Que tal! Bien. ¿Y tu?*
ALICIA. No way! *¡PAPI!* What is that?

(DAD enters.)

DAD. *Cabeza de Chivo.*
ALICIA. DAD! IT'S A GOAT HEAD!
DAD. *Cabeza de Chivo.*
GOAT HEAD. He said, *Cabeza de Chivo.* Don't you hear well? *(DAD takes a fork and plucks out one eye and eats it.)* OUCH! *Como dicen aqui.*
DAD. The eye is the best part. At the ranch, we fought for the eyes. Here you have the other.
GOAT HEAD. Go ahead and take my other eye. Go ahead. I dare you. Have a blind goat on your conscience.
DAD. Here. Have the eye. It's so good.
GOAT HEAD. After the eyes, you might as well go for my brains. *(Pause.)* Well? Do what your father tells you. *(ALICIA takes a fork and walks up to the GOAT in the oven. She drops the fork.)*
ALICIA. I can't eat eyes!
GOAT HEAD. Eat my brains then! God knows you need 'em.
ALICIA. Ramon!
RAMON. It's like head cheese.
ALICIA. NO! I don't eat brains.

GOAT HEAD. You have to obey your father. Do what your father says. Then make a burrito out of my tongue.
DAD. The tongue tastes so good in a burrito.
ALICIA. No. I can't eat goat head. What's happening?
RAMON. The land of memory? Maybe.
ALICIA. It's the squished horny toad!

(From behind the stove comes a man-size HORNY TOAD. His tongue zips out and grabs hold of ALICIA's fork and takes the goat eye and swallows it. ALICIA backs away.)

DAD. Where are you going, *hija?* Oh, don't tell me this bothers you? We ate everything on the ranch. What's the matter-you? What's the matter-you?
GOAT HEAD, HORNY TOAD, DAD *(hook up and sing)*. What's the matter you—HEY—What's the matter you—HEY—What's the matter you—HEY? *(They disappear.)*
ALICIA. Ramon! What's happening to me? Where are we?
RAMON. Did the goat head really talk to you in your kitchen?
ALICIA. You mean back then?
RAMON. *Si.*
ALICIA. No. It did now, though.
RAMON. I think maybe we are in the Distorted Memory Forest.
ALICIA. The what?
RAMON. Where a memory becomes real, but in a stranger way.
ALICIA. I remember my dad cooking a goat head, and insisting I taste an eye, but that was all.
RAMON. It didn't sing to you?
ALICIA. No.
RAMON. What about the horny toad?

ALICIA. I guess from the story of when my grandmother killed it with a brick. I was really young when this all happened.
RAMON. You want to leave?
ALICIA. Yes.

(A BOX with legs enters and exits.)

ALICIA. What was that?
RAMON. Something from your memory again?
ALICIA. A box with legs? I don't recall that.
RAMON. Maybe it's your future.
ALICIA *(unsure)*. No.

(Suddenly a brown box is dropped on the stage. ALICIA turns and walks to it. She circles it and then walks away. The gang of ELVIRAS run across the stage with chicken claws. ALICIA hides behind the box. She decides to open it. Plastic stuffing erupts from it. She sticks her hands into the box and pulls out a goat skull. The goat skull has long eyelashes similar to ROSA's. ALICIA screams and run. RAMON chases after her. They run together until it gets very dark. RAMON finally stops. ALICIA falls to the ground.)

RAMON. Are you okay?
ALICIA. Yes.
RAMON. The goat skull with the long eyelashes scared you?
ALICIA. YES. *(Pause.)* I wonder if the Elvira gang is after Rosa.
RAMON. Who's Rosa?
ALICIA. She was this doll I saw at the store. She grew large and every time I see her, she runs away.

RAMON. Let's get going to the temple.
ALICIA. All right. But I hope this is it with the memory business. I don't like looking back. *(They start to walk on a path, RAMON is untangling himself from his strings. They stop for ALICIA to help him. They hear strange sounds.)*
RAMON. *¿Sabes que?*
ALICIA. What?
RAMON. I'm scared of that noise.
ALICIA. What do you think it is?
RAMON. This time I don't know the answer. Could you hurry?
ALICIA. I'm trying. You have a big knot.
RAMON. *Pronto. Pronto.*
ALICIA. I'm trying. I need something to loosen this knot. I'll cut a little branch from that tree over there.
RAMON. Look at that tree!

(ALICIA looks up and sees a tree full of heads. One head is a MAMBO KING. Another head is CHARO. Another is PONCHO VILLA. Another head is a PACHUCO. The last head is a HISPANIC YUPPIE. The heads look about.)

RAMON. *It's a stereotype scrambler!!!!*
CHARO HEAD. *Cuchi, cuchi.*
RAMON. Ask them if we are headed to the Aztec temple.
ALICIA. All right. You're not afraid, are you?
RAMON. Of course not. I'll stay here. I'll keep an eye out for Rosa.
ALICIA *(walks to the tree)*. Hello. Excuse me. Would you happen to know where—
PANCHO VILLA HEAD. *Vamos atacar, muchachita.*
ALICIA. I was going to ask—

MAMBO KING HEAD. Look at her down there, she's staring at us.
HISPANIC YUPPIE HEAD. Yes, she is.
ALICIA. What are you doing there?
ALL HEADS. Hanging around.
ALICIA. Are your heads on branches? Did your heads grow there?
CHARO HEAD. Joo ask too meny queshans.
ALICIA. I've only asked four.
PACHUCO HEAD. That's right. She's only asked four questions.
ALICIA. Who are you?
PANCHO VILLA HEAD. *Son cinco preguntas, mi generale.*
MAMBO KING HEAD. Who are we? Well, we're your incarnations.
HISPANIC YUPPIE HEAD. What you will be, after you go. *(Turns to other HEAD.)* Is that right?
ALICIA. When I'm dead, or when I pass by?
CHARO HEAD. *Cuchi, cuchi.*
PACHUCO HEAD. Stop shaking the tree, man.
CHARO HEAD. I like to shake. *Cuchi, cuchi.*
PANCHO VILLA HEAD. *Mi, generale,* tell her the truth.
MAMBO KING HEAD. What kind of truth do you want me to tell her?
HISPANIC YUPPIE HEAD. The truth is so fabulous. Go on, I elect you to tell her.
CHARO HEAD. *Cuchi, cuchi.* The truth is, is, is. I forgot the truth...What is the truth?
PACHUCO HEAD. The truth, bimbo head.
CHARO HEAD. My name is Charo.
PANCHO VILLA HEAD. *Levante la caravina Charo. Hay guerra.*
CHARO HEAD. He's insulting me, *panchito* head.

PACHUCO HEAD. Because you are lacking in brains, man.

MAMBO KING HEAD. She's waiting for an answer. Can we tell her something?

ALICIA. That's six.

MAMBO KING HEAD. Six what?

ALICIA. Seven. Seven questions. Seven for you and six for me.

HISPANIC YUPPIE HEAD. She's counting. Are you counting?

ALICIA. Eight.

HISPANIC YUPPIE HEAD. She's counting.

ALICIA. Will you answer?

CHARO HEAD. Now it's seven questions.

PACHUCO HEAD. Seven to eight, *ese*.

ALICIA. Will you stop it?

ALL HEADS. TIE!

ALICIA. Thank goodness.

PANCHO VILLA HEAD. Just tell her the truth, *muchachitos*.

ALICIA. That would be nice.

MAMBO KING HEAD. Jes, it would. Wouldn't it?

ALICIA. Broke the tie.

ALL HEADS. Let's stop.

ALICIA. Okay. You started it, though.

PANCHO VILLA HEAD. ¿*Nosotros?*

ALICIA. Didn't you?

MAMBO KING HEAD. Tie.

ALL HEADS. STOP!

ALICIA. Truce.

ALL HEADS. Truce.

PANCHO VILLA HEAD. We are heads in a tree.

MAMBO KING HEAD. That's all we can tell you.

ALICIA. Why?

HISPANIC YUPPIE HEAD. What's the score?

Act I　　　　　(or I Can't Eat Goat Head)　　　　Page 25

CHARO HEAD. We'll tell you at the end.

HISPANIC YUPPIE HEAD. Okay. That will be so swell, *amigo.*

PACHUCO HEAD. I'll tell her who we are, *simon.* [pronounced: see-moan] We are—

PANCHO VILLA HEAD. Thoughts.

ALICIA. Thoughts?

PACHUCO HEAD. That sounded good, man. We are your thoughts.

ALICIA. How can you be my thoughts?

MAMBO KING HEAD. Okay. We're your memories, then.

ALICIA. Which is it?

ALL HEADS. Thoughts.

HISPANIC YUPPIE HEAD. With a dash of memories.

CHARO HEAD. And hope.

PACHUCO HEAD. And disappointment.

PANCHO VILLA HEAD. *Muchachita,* we're also your—

ALICIA *(overlapping).* Stop! I've had enough. And I've had more than my fill with memories.

MAMBO KING HEAD. If you are confused, then walk around the tree three times, and you'll see the truth.

RAMON. Don't do it!

ALICIA. I'm going to do it. Oh, my! *(Lights shift. She begins walking around the tree.)* I see lizards...

(ROSA appears and mouths ALICIA's words from a distance.)

ALICIA. ...on the sand. Snakes sunbathing on the side of the road. It's very warm. There is something about a desert that most people don't realize. You may see a new blade of grass in a spot where it wasn't before. A rock moved from one place to another by a passing coyote. Sniffing next to it for a moment. Crickets with only one leg will hobble across the sand. It's those differences that intrigue me each time I go across...a desert. And the colors.

ROSA *(with ALICIA mouthing the words)*. The colors of the desert change from each minute of the day. I sometimes would sit and watch these differences change before my eyes. The morning brings colors that can't even be described. They can't be described because there is a certain feeling that it gives you when it changes. And it's lost. In seconds, with the minutes, with the hours of the day. As soon as you try to explain the feeling, the colors in the sky and the landscape have already changed, and the feeling changed, too. The blade of grass has dried up and died, and next to it, another foolish blade of grass takes its place. Spreading the inside of the leaf towards the sun. Following it with its gloss as it goes across the sky, and then, down into the mountains, where new colors and feelings scream at you...*(She walks around the tree again.)*

ALICIA. On a very hot day, where all the colors around me burn my eyes and heat up my brain—Oh, my head hurts.

RAMON. The tree is making her aware!

ALICIA *(walking around the tree again)*. The grass has turned brown and the sand has turned yellow. The tongues of the coyotes and vultures have turned deep red. I saw Mexican souls walking far in the desert. Or are they from Peru, or El Salvador? Headed to the farms looking for work. I wanted to tell them they were going the wrong way, but I didn't want to destroy their mission. All day I thought about the dried blades of grass.

HISPANIC YUPPIE HEAD. Awesome.

MAMBO KING HEAD. Too long.

CHARO HEAD. I liked it. *Cuchi, cuchi.*

ALICIA. Ramon, what did that all mean?

Act I   (or I Can't Eat Goat Head)   Page 27

RAMON. Ah, don't you know? *(Sees ROSA.)* Alicia! Look over there. Is that her? I think I see Rosa.

(ROSA's and ALICIA's eyes meet. ROSA then motions for the box with legs to enter. It does so and goes towards ALICIA. ALICIA starts to open it. She takes out some Mexican pottery. ROSA disappears.)

CHARO HEAD. The box has a pottery in it.
HISPANIC YUPPIE HEAD. Eat beans out of Mexican pottery. It makes 'em taste better. The *frijoles* they serve at the restaurants are canned!
ALL HEADS. YECH!
MAMBO KING HEAD. What's the count?
PANCHO VILLA HEAD. We got thirteen, she has fourteen.
CHARO HEAD. Who was that beautiful lady?
ALL HEADS. TIE!
ALICIA. She's trying to make me follow her. I don't know. Let's go, Ramon.
RAMON. What about the Aztec temple?
ALICIA. I have to find her.
RAMON. *Entonces, vamanos. (A wind blows through. Hair spray cans roll onstage.)*
ALICIA. What is this?
RAMON. Aye, ya yai. Looks like hair spray. Smells like hair spray. Feels like hair spray. Tastes like hair spray. The Elvira gang must be around here, teasing and spraying their hair until it's a stiff mass! I heard they put staples in their hair, so if you grab it, your hand will get cut. I'm getting out of here. *(RAMON exits running.)*
ALICIA. Wait! Ramon! *(The odor of hair spray is overwhelming. ALICIA pinches her nose.)* Ramon!

(The ELVIRAS are heard in the background. ARMADILLA appears, takes ALICIA's hand and pulls her into a crevice. They hide there until the ELVIRAS appear, spraying and teasing their hair. They then pass by.)

ARMADILLA *(Texas accent continues).* You have a brain in that head of yours?

ALICIA. Ramon ran off. I have to find him.

ARMADILLA. Just stay close. I think the Elviras will come back soon. You've walked onto their territory. Come on. I'll take you through a short cut.

ALICIA. His strings must really be tangled up now. He ran so fast.

ARMADILLA. And that wind didn't help either. *(They enter a dark room and smoke comes out of a corner.)* Well, I'll be. It's *abuelita*. *(A cigarette is seen in the darkness. Smoke comes from it.)* She's over there in the darkness of my memory. *(She looks at the smoke.)* *Abuelita* liked to smoke...I remember when *abuelita* came to stay with us. She wouldn't say very much. She just nodded when I talked to her...¿*Abuelita, te gusta fumar? (Smoke blows out of the darkness.)* She never wanted anything. Just a smoke. Her withered brown body, sucking on a cigarette for survival.

ALICIA. Is this story about your grandmother?

ARMADILLA. *Abuela*! Don't you know Spanish? Aren't you bilingual? *(Pause.)* It's a Mexican Cinderella story with a sad ending. All stories in Mexico have sad endings. Don't you ever see Mexican movies? The ones they make now are not sad enough. The ones made in the '30s and '40s were just right. All you have to do when you need to cheer yourself up is to compare sad stories. *(ARMADILLA sees a spot.)* Did you see that? I thought I saw a spot. I'm on to something...Her hair was a simple braid. She was petite with

Act I (or I Can't Eat Goat Head) Page 29

light green eyes. Always, one hand on her hip, and the other holding what happened to her life, a cigarette...*(She sees the spot get larger.)* I felt her quiet despair. *(The spot gets even larger.)* I remember asking her when she started to smoke. She told me it was in 1913. She was once a daughter of a rich man. She even had her own servant to brush her hair, to choose the clothes she was to wear, and bring her *cafe y pan dulce*. Her servant took care of her. Even after her mother died. *(The spot fades away.)* Then, then the servant decided she wanted *abuelita's* father for herself. He had no plans to remarry. He had to travel. New tracks were being laid out in Mexico in the turn of the century and he was in charge of the plans. He left his daughter in the care of the servant. She was an aristocrat, they say. *(The spot returns.)* There was an Indian peasant who worked in her lush gardens. *(Smoke comes out of the darkness.)* One day, her father returned to the wailing of the servant. She said that his precious daughter was in the company of the gardener in the dark of the nights. She suspected that they were lovers, and that she was absolutely sure she was not pure anymore. *(Smoke comes out of the darkness.)* The father got a gun and held it to the gardener's head. He was going to—

WOMAN'S VOICE *(from the darkness)*. ¡NO PAPÁ! ¡NO ES CIERTO! ¡POR EL AMOR DE DIOS! It's not true!

ARMADILLA. —Or, restore family honor by marrying his daughter. *(The spots jump around.)* She married him—to save his life. The well-bred daughter became the wife of a man who could barely put dinner on the table. *(Cigarette smoke comes out of the darkness.)*

ALICIA *(overlapping)*. But—

ARMADILLA *(overlapping)*. —SHH! The spot is staying. Yes. Faded years and children later—oh, and cut out of the family fortune—her aging father found out the truth.

ALICIA. The truth?

ARMADILLA. He had to rescue her from the poor life he forced her to live. He found out she was trapped in a lie.

ALICIA. Did the servant confess?

ARMADILLA. Yes, and not only that, she lost her mind over the years with the lie. That's what happens when you lie. You suffer from it. She also had the disappointment of the lie not even working. He didn't marry her. All these years, he was committed *only* to his first wife.

ALICIA. How many years?

ARMADILLA. Many years. This wouldn't be a sad story if it didn't have years wasted. He was already a very old man. He immediately boarded the train. Sickness of heart and mind for convicting his only daughter to death in a marriage she didn't belong...And when he arrived, as Mexican luck would have it, he had a heart attack, and died on the train. *(Cigarette smoke is blown out of the darkness.)*

ALICIA. He didn't make it?

ARMADILLA. Nope. Mexican luck. I said that, didn't I?

ALICIA. It was too late?

ARMADILLA. Everything in this story was too late. Don't you listen well?

ALICIA. Why didn't he believe her at the beginning?

ARMADILLA. A rich man's world. Anyhow, it doesn't matter. He finally realized what he had done. Just too, too late. It wouldn't have mattered. He ignored her for too many years. She already had borne fourteen children. Seven of which died in her accepted poverty. She dressed like a peasant, but hid in the darkness when well-bred women were close by. She knew she was supposed to be like them in finer clothing, but had bad luck. *(The cigarette is tossed on the floor and put out. The spot fades away.)*

Act I (or I Can't Eat Goat Head) Page 31

ALICIA. This is such a sad story. Why do you even think about it?

ARMADILLA. Being fatalistic is part of the culture!

ALICIA. Doesn't have to be.

ARMADILLA. Where are you from? Did you see any more spots during the story? Looks like they all left. Hey, watch out for that maraca pit. *(They stand in front of a maraca pit.)* Ever buy a maraca and don't know what to do with it? That's where they end up. In the maraca pit.

ALICIA. There's so many!

ARMADILLA. You buy 'em, get bored, toss it away and it ends up here. Maraca heaven. *(ARMADILLA starts to exit.)*

ALICIA. Where are you going?

ARMADILLA. Just over here. Gotta catch me some spots.

ALICIA. Wait!

RAMON *(off)*. Let go of me.

CACTUS MAN *(off)*. Let go of me.

(ALICIA goes through a garden then sees RAMON's strings tangled on a prickly pear cactus bush. The CACTUS has a head and arms and red fruit [tunas] on it.)

CACTUS MAN. Get your strings off of me.

RAMON. The wind blew me here. Ouch, ouch, ouch, ouch.

CACTUS MAN. Get off of me.

ALICIA. Ramon!

RAMON. Alicia! Help me. Ouch, ouch, ouch. He thinks I did this on purpose. Ouch, ouch, ouch.

CACTUS MAN. I'm tired of being bothered. If it's not a puppet bothering me, it's a herd of tortoise.

ALICIA. Tortoise?

CACTUS MAN. Tortoise. Take him off of me. TAKE HIM OFF OF ME. At least you don't bite like those annoying desert turtles. *(ALICIA starts untangling RAMON from CACTUS MAN.)*

ALICIA. Ouch, ouch, ouch.

RAMON. Ouch, ouch, ouch.

CACTUS MAN. Each year when my *tunas* [pronounced: thnoonas], that's this fruit, grows, turtles want to eat them. You'd think my needles would protect me. They do, but not from the tortoises. They have strong jaws.

RAMON. *Pobrecito nopal.*

ALICIA. Must be good fruit.

CACTUS MAN. Of course they're good, but who says I want them bitten off me. Are you done, yet?

ALICIA. Almost. Ouch, ouch, ouch. There. *(RAMON comes off of CACTUS MAN.)*

CACTUS MAN. Good. Finally. At last. Can you do me a favor? Scare off the turtles before they make me unattractive. They keep putting bite marks on me and causing me to scar. They should wait until I drop the *tunas* down. They're so impatient.

ALICIA. Then why don't you do that?

CACTUS MAN. Do what?

ALICIA. Drop the *tunas* on the ground so they don't have to reach up and scar you.

CACTUS MAN. Say what?

ALICIA. Shake yourself and the *tunas* will fall. They'll just pick 'em up and take 'em away. They won't chew on you anymore.

RAMON. That's a good idea.

CACTUS MAN. I'll just shake right now and see if it works. *(CACTUS MAN shakes and all the* tunas *fall off.)* It works.

ALICIA. Ouch. I have needles in my hand.

CACTUS MAN. Sorry.

Act I   (or I Can't Eat Goat Head)   Page 33

ALICIA. Mr. Cactus. We're in a hurry. Which way out of here?
CACTUS MAN. Well, since you helped me solve my problem, *that way.*
ALICIA. Are you sure?
CACTUS MAN. Well, I don't get out much, but that's the direction.
ALICIA. Thanks.
RAMON. Let's go Alicia. Adios, Mr. Pin Cushion.
CACTUS MAN. I'm Cactus Man. Don't forget that. *(ALICIA and RAMON exit. CACTUS MAN shakes and smiles.)* Dinner time. Come and get it! Ah, I feel ten pounds lighter. *(He shakes again. He looks up.)* How come that eagle has a snake in his mouth? Hey, don't land on me! *(Blackout.)*

SCENE THREE

AT RISE: *ARMADILLA on a sofa. Her eyes stare straight out. HORNY TOAD enters with his tongue hanging out.*

ARMADILLA. You have a saliva problem or something? Keep your slimy tongue off me. You have a problem?
HORNY TOAD. No.
ARMADILLA. Then keep your bodily fluids to yourself. What do you think you are—a waterfall?
HORNY TOAD. No.
ARMADILLA. Where is she?
HORNY TOAD. I don't know.
ARMADILLA. Go away, you bother me. I said scram. What's wrong with you? Get your tongue off of me, will you? Boy, I wish I had a brick.

HORNY TOAD. But I'm harmless.

ARMADILLA. You look like the devil.

HORNY TOAD. I've been called that, but I'm not. I'm just an ugly fellow. I feel sorry for myself sometimes.

ARMADILLA. You got horns all over you.

HORNY TOAD. I know.

ARMADILLA. Look at that tail.

HORNY TOAD. I'm ashamed of it.

ARMADILLA. You are?

HORNY TOAD. Mostly when someone points it out.

ARMADILLA. Sorry. I'm a little edgy today.

HORNY TOAD. Why?

ARMADILLA. I miss my spots.

HORNY TOAD. Staring at the sun is bad for your eyes.

ARMADILLA. Not you, too! You like the sun, don't you?

HORNY TOAD. Yes. Every time I sit in the sun school kids want to take me to school. I'll sit in the sun until one decides to take me to class. That's when I feel important. I feel like they're admiring who I really am. Some look at me and think I'm ugly. Everyone looking and thinking that I'm ugly, makes me ugly...But when someone thinks I'm okay, I'm okay. *(Pause.)* It's all on how they treat you.

ARMADILLA. I'm sorry to get you all emotional.

HORNY TOAD. There are people who go through life just to hurt you. Sometimes it's better to let them break you down quickly so they'll go away sooner. Then, you'll wrestle with your pain in peace.

ARMADILLA. HEY!!!!!! WATCH OUT! *(A huge brick falls on the HORNY TOAD. He lies there flat.)* Hey! Hey! Are you all right? Hey? Does it hurt? Get up. Get up, you toad. I was just beginning to like you.

HORNY TOAD *(getting up)*. You were?

ARMADILLA. Are you okay?

Act I   (or I Can't Eat Goat Head)   Page 35

HORNY TOAD. That's the fifth time today. I'm getting used to it, though. If it's not a brick landing on me it's a—

(PANCHO VILLA HEAD falls from the Tree of Heads.)

HORNY TOAD. —A head. Look what came down on me this time. Pancho Villa!
PANCHO VILLA HEAD. You better believe it.
ARMADILLA. Get a basket. It's almost harvest time.
HORNY TOAD. Is it ripe?
ARMADILLA. Must be. It fell out of the tree.
PANCHO VILLA HEAD. *Fue un accidente, muchachitos.*
HORNY TOAD. Hey, do you hear somebody?

(The ELVIRAS and ROSA appear. The ELVIRAS stomp and clap a haunting rhythm and surround ROSA.)

HORNY TOAD. Oh, my gosh! See that?
ARMADILLA. Time to go.
HORNY TOAD. What do we do? *(The ELVIRAS continue threatening ROSA.)* We got to help her.
ARMADILLA. What? And get a chicken claw in our back? *(The ELVIRAS continue threatening in a rhythmic manner.)*
ELVIRA #1. Chicken claw.
ELVIRA #2. Chicken claw.
ELVIRA #3. Chicken claw.
ELVIRA #4. Chicken claw. *(HORNY TOAD can't stand it anymore and throws the PANCHO VILLA HEAD at the ELVIRAS.)*
PANCHO VILLA HEAD. *Shing-ga-do!* [pronounced: Sheeng-ga-doe] *(The HEAD flies in the air and lands in the hands of ELVIRA #1.)*
ELVIRA #1. Who is this?

ELVIRA #2. I don't know.

PANCHO VILLA HEAD. You are not fit to live if you don't know who I am. I'm Pancho Villa!

ELVIRA #3. Get rid of it. *(ELVIRA #1 throws the HEAD off.)*

PANCHO VILLA HEAD. *Que mala suerteeeeeee.* *(ROSA tries to escape but the ELVIRAS keep her from moving.)*

ROSA. What do you want with me?

ELVIRA #1. We want your culture.

ELVIRA #2. We want your roots.

ELVIRA #3. We want your spine.

ELVIRA #4. And if we can't have it.

ALL ELVIRAS. NO ONE CAN!

ELVIRA #1. Tie her up.

ELVIRA #2. Tie her to this stupid Tree of Heads. *(The HEADS shake in fright.)*

MAMBO KING HEAD. Learn some respect.

ELVIRA #3. Shut up or we'll cut you all off.

ELVIRA #4. And eat you.

ELVIRA #1. You saw what we did to the other head.

HISPANIC YUPPIE HEAD. Hey. *No problemas.* You got it. *(The HEADS clench their lips.)*

ELVIRA #1. Tie her to the tree. When that girl comes here, we'll grab her.

ELVIRA #2. Then we can get her.

ELVIRA #3. And make her into one of us.

ELVIRA #4. After we strip her of all identity.

ALL ELVIRAS. Yeah. Like it was done to us. *(The ELVIRAS exit in haunting stomps. When they are gone, ARMADILLA and HORNY TOAD approach.)*

ROSA. Please. Don't come any closer. They are not too far off.

ARMADILLA. Are you all right?

PACHUCO HEAD. It's a trap. The Elvira gang wants Alicia.

HISPANIC YUPPIE HEAD. They want to keep her from finding her roots.
CHARO HEAD. From finding her *self*.
PACHUCO HEAD. Just troublemakers, that's what they are.
MAMBO KING HEAD. They want to keep her from having a good time.
HORNY TOAD. Is there anything we can do?
ROSA. Find Alicia and tell her to find the Aztec temple.
ARMADILLA. Can we help you get out of there?
ROSA. This is my fate. At least Alicia can be saved. Go.
ARMADILLA. I know fate very well. All right. We'll find her. Come on, Horny.
ROSA. Hurry before the Elvira gang finds her. They'll try to prevent her from finding the answers. Hurry.
HORNY TOAD. We'll do our best to find her. Come on, Armadilla.
ARMADILLA. Since when did you become boss?
HORNY TOAD. Now?

(They exit. Suddenly the ELVIRAS enter.)

ROSA. She's going to make it.
ALL ELVIRAS *(hiss)*. S-s-s-s-s-s-s. *(Blackout.)*

SCENE FOUR

AT RISE: *Darkness. In the distance we barely see ALICIA and RAMON running. They fade into the lights slowly. They are running in figure eights and holding hands. Then, on the other side, we see ARMADILLA and HORNY TOAD doing the same thing, but falling and tripping over. They **continue running in figure eights going the opposite direc-***

tion. Eventually ALICIA and RAMON enlarge their figure eight and ARMADILLA and HORNY TOAD run in it, still in the opposite direction. They don't notice each other until HORNY TOAD stops and RAMON crashes into him. Then ALICIA crashes into ARMADILLA and they all scream and run different directions. ARMADILLA and HORNY TOAD exit screaming.

ALICIA. Wait a minute.
RAMON. *¿Que te pasa?*
ALICIA. Are they looking for Rosa?
RAMON. *Que carajo. Mira mi trompeta.*
ALICIA. Come on. We don't have time to waste.
RAMON *(toots his horn and is more disgusted).* You suppose this pottery maker can make a new trumpet for me? I don't mind if it's made out of ceramic or clay. My head and hands are made of ceramic. Then painted. See this mustache of mine. It's not real. It's painted.
ALICIA. It's kind of sloppy.
RAMON. It's called *art*. Maybe when you grow up, you'll be cultured.
ALICIA. What's that supposed to mean?
RAMON. *Aye, Caray.*
ALICIA. What?
RAMON. Look over there, *niña.*
ALICIA. A black wall.
RAMON. Feel it.
ALICIA. Feels very soft.
RAMON. It's velvet.
ALICIA. Oh, black velvet. How pretty. I once had a dress made with velvet.
RAMON. Excuse me.
ALICIA. What?

RAMON. We're not in the Memory Forest. We are in the maze of the velvet paintings.

ALICIA. Velvet paintings? I've seen velvet paintings in Tiajuana at the bazaars.

RAMON. You do a lot of shopping, don't you? *(They walk by a huge velvet painting of a beautiful tiger. It hisses at them. RAMON gasps.)* Took my breath away. *(They pass an Elvis velvet painting. He strums his guitar.)*

(ELVIS. Thank you, thank you very much.)

RAMON. *Orale, Elvis. Toca la guitara otra vez.* *(They pass by a velvet painting of a matador and a bull.)*

ALICIA. *Toro. Toro.*

RAMON. Roll your "r" a little.

ALICIA. I did.

RAMON. No you didn't. *(The bull snorts and then comes out of the painting. ALICIA and RAMON start to run. They go in and out of the velvet painting maze. Finally they outrun the bull and find themselves resting in front of the Aztec temple.)* Hijole.

ALICIA. Is it the Aztec temple?

RAMON. You better believe it.

ALICIA. The pottery maker!

RAMON. *Busca una puerta.*

ALICIA. Look, a *piñata.*

RAMON. Of course. *La piñata.* There are special things inside *piñatas.* The way we do a *piñata*—

ALICIA *(interrupting).* I know, I know. I'm not that out of touch. *(RAMON takes a blindfold and puts it on ALICIA. He then gives her a bat. He twirls her around and around and around and around. Then he twirls her again and she goes around and around and around.)* All right, already.

RAMON. Sorry. *(He taps the end of the bat on the side of the* piñata *and signals for ALICIA to begin swinging. The* piñata *goes up and down and all over the place as she swings the bat. ALICIA, in frustration, stops. Her one eye is peeking over the blindfold. She sees the* piñata *and breaks it to pieces. A shower of candy comes from all directions. RAMON and ALICIA pick up the candy and start throwing it back, in all directions. One big piece of candy falls on RAMON's head. ALICIA picks it up.)*

ALICIA. There's a note on this one.

RAMON. What does it say?

ALICIA. "Come-tee-es-tee-dools."

RAMON. *Comete este dulce.* It says to eat the candy.

ALICIA. Oh.

RAMON. You got to learn some Spanish.

ALICIA. Tastes good...*(Her legs begin to grow.)* Oh, no! Oh, look at my long legs!

RAMON. You could be a great dancer.

ALICIA. Hey, I'm twelve feet tall and there's a window up here.

RAMON. Oh, good. That's the way in. Grab me. *(ALICIA reaches down and pulls RAMON up by his strings. He twists and turns and goes straight up. He then is popped through the window. ALICIA is staring at him from the outside.)*

ALICIA. And how am I supposed to get in?

RAMON. You should see this place. Nice hieroglyphics.

ALICIA. Looks like graffiti.

RAMON. It's not. It's ancient handwriting.

ALICIA. Find something to make my legs shrink back to size.

RAMON *(goes to a refrigerator, pulls out a banana).* How about this?

ALICIA. It's just a banana.

RAMON. It's good for you. Potassium.

ALICIA. Find something else. We're in a hurry.

Act I (or I Can't Eat Goat Head) Page 41

RAMON. ¿Piña?

ALICIA. It has to be a potion.

RAMON. It has vitamin C.

ALICIA. Find something else.

RAMON. Mangoes. Papayas.

ALICIA. Find something with a note on it like the candy.

RAMON. Let's see now. There's some *tortillas* in there. Should I make you a *quesadilla*?

ALICIA. Come on. I'm getting cramps in my legs.

RAMON. Oh no. I get it. Get in.

ALICIA. What?

RAMON. Get in stretch. The candy effect must be for a little while. It's only temporary.

ALICIA. These legs will shrink back to size?

RAMON. *Si*, flamingo legs. Your stretched out legs will get small very soon. The effect is only temporary so you can get in. That's the idea. Hurry! Put yourself over on your stomach and lift your legs, or you'll shrink back to size without getting in. *(She does this and suddenly the legs make a strange noise, and spring back to size. ALICIA is thrust inside the room.)*

ALICIA. Weird. What are you doing?

RAMON *(preoccupied at the refrigerator)*. Looking for a Coca Cola.

ALICIA. Let's go.

(They go through a door. SUGAR SKULL is in the way preventing their passage.)

SUGAR SKULL. *Perdon.*

ALICIA. The Day of the Dead sugar skull.

SUGAR SKULL. You better believe it. And who is this?

ALICIA. Ramon.

SUGAR SKULL. Ramon. Roll your r's. Where are you both going?

ALICIA. We need answers.

SUGAR SKULL. We all do, but do we get them? NO. So should we ask them? NO.

ALICIA. If I remember correctly, sugar skulls taste real good.

SUGAR SKULL. You said you never had one.

ALICIA. But I know they taste good.

SUGAR SKULL. How do you know?

ALICIA. Look at all the colors on your skull. Orange, yellow, pink. Layer after layer of sweet sugar. Ribbons of color coiling around. You even glisten with sweetness.

SUGAR SKULL *(melting with the compliments)*. You really think so?

ALICIA. Oh, yes.

SUGAR SKULL. Where were you going?

ALICIA. To ask the Aztec priest a very important question.

SUGAR SKULL. Be my guest. Do I really glisten?

ALICIA. Like a rainbow on snow. *(SUGAR SKULL allows ALICIA and RAMON to pass.)*

SUGAR SKULL. What a wonderful girl.

(SUGAR SKULL, ALICIA and RAMON enter a majestic room. An ornately-dressed AZTEC PRIEST enters, wearing a magnificent headdress. He is staring blankly as drums beat with his grand entrance. The event is spectacular.)

ALICIA and RAMON. It's the Aztec Priest! *(Long moment.)*

END OF ACT ONE

ACT TWO

SCENE ONE

ALICIA and RAMON *(repeating last line from end of Act One)*. It's the Aztec Priest!

ALICIA. Are you the Aztec priest?

AZTEC PRIEST *(mysterious, then like Don Rickles or having Jewish accent)*. Yeah. One of them. The rest are on vacation, my little feather serpent. *(To RAMON.)* Hey, what's with the strings? Your mother ever teach you to floss properly?

ALICIA. We came to ask you if you could direct us to the pottery maker. *(RAMON is looking at all the strange things situated for observation in the Aztec room.)*

RAMON. Hey, look at all the toys.

AZTEC PRIEST. Toys? Toys? These are technological advances, and pretty cool stuff. I'm keeping an eye on them. In case someone wants to make off with them. *(To RAMON.)* Take your hands off the merchandise. I otta smack you one. Hey, you peg-head, get atta here.

ALICIA. What's in those scrolls?

AZTEC PRIEST *(suspicious)*. If you are from Spain, you better keep your hands in your pockets. I remember the last time. Who was that guy? Oh, yeah, called himself Cortez.

ALICIA. I'm not from Spain.

AZTEC PRIEST. Oh, then come over here. Leave that knucklehead with the bad make-up job over there. You make me nervous, wood man. Now these scrolls have written on them technological advances of the Aztec Empire.

The Spanish didn't get their hands on these. They were only interested in gold. See that flower in the vase? It has been alive for nearly a year. Hear that, you weak-kneed pinocchio? Who taught you how to walk? You need an orthopedic surgeon? My uncle can do miracles for you. I have his card somewhere. Dr. Kaufman. But seriously, folks.

RAMON. Can we get back to task?

AZTEC PRIEST. A wise guy. Getting smart with me. See that dagger? It's curved to take the heart out, in three seconds.

RAMON. Take the heart out of what?

AZTEC PRIEST. Out of humans, you meatball. The heart is still pounding in your hand when you take it out at the sacrifice. It helps keep the sun god happy. We must placate the gods, or else.

RAMON. Or else, what?

AZTEC PRIEST. Or else, some disaster will befall us. Like... bad weather. Stay with me.

ALICIA. Who gets sacrificed?

AZTEC PRIEST. Are you interested?

ALICIA. Of course not.

AZTEC PRIEST. Just doing my job. I'm a working Aztec priest. My wife wants rings for all her fingers and toes. My sons are out carving the ground trying to signal extra-terrestrials.

ALICIA. About the sacrifices.

AZTEC PRIEST. Oh, yeah. Well, we find the most beautiful person to sacrifice. But recently, we ran out of good-looking people. Are you sure you're not interested? We'd build a stone shrine for you.

ALICIA. No. I'm not interested. But let's think about that for a moment. You took good-looking people?

Act II (or I Can't Eat Goat Head) Page 45

AZTEC PRIEST. Yes.

ALICIA. The ugly ones get to live.

AZTEC PRIEST. It's a compliment to be sacrificed and a public service.

ALICIA. I think that's mean.

AZTEC PRIEST. It's tradition.

ALICIA. Well, it has to stop.

AZTEC PRIEST. It did. Too many ugly people—And over there, on that slab of dry clay, is the way we calculated many things like taxes, rent, we counted animals, etc., etc. And there is our great calendar. We beat out the Egyptians on many scientific advances.

RAMON. And what is this? *(RAMON stares at the wall. It is reflecting his image.)*

AZTEC PRIEST. That's a sheet of gold, polished to reflect your image. In other words, a mirror. *(ALICIA looks into the mirror and sees images of an Aztec village in progress.)*

ALICIA. Who are those people?

AZTEC PRIEST. It's the Aztec community. They are going about their daily business.

ALICIA. It's like a magic window. *(Suddenly the mirror shows an image of ARMADILLA and HORNY TOAD running.)* Oh, look, it's Armadilla and Horny Toad.

AZTEC PRIEST. Oh, yeah. I saw them before. They look like Spanish spies.

ALICIA. They're not spies. Why are they running?

AZTEC PRIEST. Who do you think I am? Quetzalcoatl? If you want to know that you better ask the pottery maker.

ALICIA and RAMON. The pottery maker????

AZTEC PRIEST. That's what I said, the pottery maker. Next door to your right.

ALICIA. Well, that's what we are here for.

AZTEC PRIEST. Then, next door to your right.

(ALICIA and RAMON go through a door and see beautiful pottery all over. The room illuminates to an unearthly glow. Suddenly SOULS come out of the pottery and dance before them. Note: Use the specified accents throughout.)

ALICIA. Ramon, look! Are they ghosts?
SOUL #1 *(French accent)*. We are souls.
SOUL #2 *(Cockney accent)*. We are souls waiting.
SOUL #3 *(Italian accent)*. We are souls waiting for—
SOUL #4 *(Hebrew accent)*. Deliverance.
ALICIA. Souls waiting for deliverance?
SOUL #1. Souls waiting for life above.
SOUL #2. Souls waiting for life above where—
SOUL #3. There is peace.
ALICIA. Peace? Aren't you at peace now?
SOUL #4. Yeah, but we like to complain.
SOUL #1. So we are here.
SOUL #2. Waiting.
SOUL #3. Waiting.
SOUL #4. Waiting.
SOUL #1 *(pause)*. Waiting.
SOUL #2. Just waiting.
RAMON. Don't wait too long. You'll miss the train.
ALL SOULS. Train? *(Sound of train. The SOULS look at each other.)*
SOUL #3. No train. We're waiting for the final place. We don't mind the wait.
ALICIA. Where's the final place?
SOUL #4. You are interrupting our dancing.
ALICIA. Well, that's because I'm looking for someone and I was told he would be here.

Act II   (or I Can't Eat Goat Head)   Page 47

SOUL #1. Who are you looking for?

ALICIA. I'm looking for the pottery maker.

SOUL #2. She's looking for the one who made our pottery, our homes.

ALL SOULS (*still dancing*). OH.

SOUL #1. Well. We could tell you where the pottery maker is.

ALICIA. You can?

SOUL #3. Don't make it easy for her.

SOUL #4. Make her sweat.

SOUL #3. Oh, fun.

SOUL #4. We'll tell you a riddle.

SOUL #1. Yes, yes. That would be fun. I'll tell her the first one. What is big and round and looks purple after you stare at it?

ALICIA. Hmm. The sun?

ALL SOULS. She got it.

SOUL #4. What has two feet and sounds like many feet when taking as few steps as possible?

RAMON. Oh, that's a hard one.

ALICIA. Hmm. A tap dancer?

SOUL #1. Think culturally.

ALICIA. Oh, a flamenco dancer.

SOUL #2. She's too smart.

SOUL #3. He gave her a clue.

SOUL #1. You didn't say I couldn't help.

SOUL #4. Oh. All right. Don't help. Here's another one. It's the last one. Get this one and we'll tell you where to find the pottery maker.

ALL SOULS. What is always better when it is broken? (*Pause.*) What is always better when it is broken?

RAMON. That's a hard one.

ALICIA. Oh, that's easy. A *piñata*.

RAMON. ¡*Que bien!*

ALL SOULS. How did you know?

ALICIA. That was easy.

SOUL #1. It's our best riddle. No one gets that one.

ALICIA. I guess the answer came to me because I went into that Mexican curio shop. It really was beautiful, though at first I was embarrassed to be there. My mother knows all about those things in the store, but I don't. There's so much to know. I see the tradition, but from afar. It's not mine, but it is. I'm expected to know the meaning of everything because of who I am, but I don't know. I have to look it up like everyone else. *(Silence.)*

ALL SOULS and RAMON. *Que lastima.*

SOUL #1. All right. She can go see the pottery maker.

ALICIA. Where is he?

SOUL #2. Next door to your right.

RAMON. *Gracias.*

ALL SOULS. *De nada.*

(The SOULS start to dance as ALICIA and RAMON exit into the next chamber where a dinner table is being set by the participants for menudo *(Mexican tripe soup). SUGAR SKULL is on the table just looking around. GOAT HEAD arrives and goes to the table. He is wearing dark glasses because he is blind now. A FLAMENCO DANCER is trying to arrange the napkins, but they keep flying off. She finally sits and starts fanning herself excessively with an over-size fan. A box with legs enters, then bursts open. Plastic foam spills out for a minute and then a VENTRILOQUIST and a DUMMY emerge. The VENTRILOQUIST is a normal-looking person. The DUMMY is a contorted Rosarita from the refried beans commercial. She has braids with ribbons weaved in, and wears a Mexican dress.)*

Act II   (or **I Can't Eat Goat Head**)   Page 49

ROSARITA REFRIED. Hey everybody, it's time for *menudo!*

VENTRILOQUIST. Be a little more quiet.

ROSARITA REFRIED. HEY, EVERYBODY, IT'S TIME FOR *MENUDO.*

FLAMENCO DANCER. Will you shut that thing up? She's going to be rude at the table again.

ROSARITA REFRIED. You're the one that's rude.

FLAMENCO DANCER *(grabs ROSARITA by the throat).* Look, you little monster, I've just about had it with you.

ROSARITA REFRIED. MAMÁ! Hey, let go of the wood.

RAMON. Hey, I'm made of wood.

ROSARITA REFRIED. You are?

RAMON. And some plaster or ceramic.

ROSARITA REFRIED. Well, which is it?

RAMON. A little of both.

ROSARITA REFRIED. Don't you know what you are made of? Who are you guys, anyway? Who invited you here?

ALICIA. We are looking for the pottery maker.

VENTRILOQUIST. The pottery maker? Did you ask the Aztec priest?

ALICIA. I did and he directed me to one chamber, and then the Souls directed me to this chamber.

ROSARITA REFRIED. Did you know I was bilingual? She isn't.

VENTRILOQUIST. I do pretty well.

ROSARITA REFRIED. Yeah, right, and mangos grow in Canada.

FLAMENCO DANCER. I want my *menudo!* Are you staying for *menudo,* or what?

ROSARITA REFRIED. See how rude she is.

VENTRILOQUIST. She's not rude. She asked in her own way if they might stay for dinner.

ROSARITA REFRIED *(sarcastic).* Ah, wasn't that nice of her. Hey, broken windmill feet, get them a bowl of *menudo.*

FLAMENCO DANCER. *(serious inhale).* Windmill feet?

ALICIA. Hey, let's be nice to each other.

SUGAR SKULL. Nice and sweet

ALICIA. It's you!

SUGAR SKULL. Where, where?

ALICIA. What are you doing here?

SUGAR SKULL. It's dinner time.

ROSARITA REFRIED. I like *menudo.* Tripe, and homily with hot sauce is so good. Add a little lemon and *cilantro, cebolla,* and we are in business.

GOAT HEAD. Personally, I like my *menudo* with rolled-up flour *tortillas,* and dipped into the soup. It's very good.

SUGAR SKULL. Corn *tortillas* are better.

GOAT HEAD. Flour *tortillas* are better.

SUGAR SKULL. Corn.

GOAT HEAD. Flour.

SUGAR SKULL. Corn.

GOAT HEAD. Flour.

SUGAR SKULL. Corn.

GOAT HEAD. Flour

SUGAR SKULL. Let's take a vote.

ALICIA. We don't have time for that.

ROSARITA REFRIED. That's right. It's time for *MENUDO!* *(FLAMENCO DANCER grabs ROSARITA's head and throws it over her shoulder.)*

FLAMENCO DANCER. Let's eat.

(The AZTEC PRIEST enters. He is wearing a fine Aztec robe and a beautiful headdress. He carries a huge pot of menudo *ceremoniously. The grand entrance is spectacular.)*

Act II   (or I Can't Eat Goat Head)   Page 51

ROSARITA REFRIED *(from afar)*. *Menudo* time.

FLAMENCO DANCER. Shut that thing up or you're next.

VENTRILOQUIST. I'm sorry. She sometimes gets out of hand.

ALICIA. I don't have time for *menudo*.

FLAMENCO DANCER. Sit down. If I can eat it, *you* can. God knows I don't eat this stuff in Spain. I'm only consenting because you have Spanish last names.

SUGAR SKULL. You like it. Don't try to be a martyr.

ALICIA. I want to find the pottery maker.

GOAT HEAD. But before we eat, we have to go around the table and sing a few bars from *"Canciones de Mi Padre,"* from the Mexican tribute album by Linda Ronstadt. What a gal.

SUGAR SKULL. Did you know Linda Ronstadt doesn't speak any Spanish?

ALL. *¡Aye caramba!*

GOAT HEAD. Give her an "A" for effort. She has a good singing voice and she selected some of my favorite rancheras for her album.

AZTEC PRIEST. I speak *Nahuatl*. My Indian tongue.

GOAT HEAD. Aye, don't say tongue.

FLAMENCO DANCER. I speak the real Spanish. *Castellano*.

SUGAR SKULL *(annoyed)*. What? And the rest of us speak *crappy* Spanish?

ALICIA. Stop! I don't get it. Why are you one-upping each other?

FLAMENCO DANCER. Because we're different.

ALICIA. Yes, we are, but we are also the same. Aren't we all human?

SUGAR SKULL. I'm made of sugar.

GOAT HEAD. I'm ready to sing a song from Ronstadt's album.

(Music begins: marachi can appear.)

> *¡Ay que laureles tan verdes!*
> *¡Que rosas tan encendidas!*
> *Si piensas abandonarme mejor quitame la vida*
> *Alza los ojos a verme*
> *Si no estas comprometido.*
>
> *Eres mata de algodon*
> *Que vives en el capullo*
> *Ay, que tristeza me da*
> *Cuando te llenas de orgullo*
> *De ver a mi corazon*
> *¡Enredado con el tuyo!*

(Spoken.) How's that my friend?

SUGAR SKULL. I know an even better one. Music, maestro.
(Music begins.)
> *Que diran los de tu casa*
> *Cuando me miren tomando.*
> *Pesaran que por tu causa*
> *Yo me vivo emborrachando, Y andale...*
> *Pero si vieras*
> *Como son lindas estas borracheras, Y andale...*

CHORUS *(most all join in).*
> *Pero hasta cuando/ Dejan tus padres de andarte*
>   *cuidando, Y andale...*

SUGAR SKULL.
> *Cada vez que vengo a verte*
> *Siempre me voy resbalando;*

O es que tengo mala suerte
O es que me esta lloviznando, Y andale...
Pero si vieras
Seco mi chaco en me higuera floreando, Y andale...

CHORUS.
Pero si cuando / Seco mi chaco en me higuera
floreando, Y andale...

SUGAR SKULL.
Me dices que soy un necio
Porque me ando emborrachando,
Y a pesar de tus desprecios,
Yo quiero seguir tomando, Y andale

Pero si vieras/ Como son lindas estas borracheras...
Y andale...

CHORUS.
Pero que bellas/ Pasos las horas vaciando botellas,
Y andale...

SUGAR SKULL.
Pero si vieras/ Como son lindas estas borracheras...
Y andale.

GOAT HEAD. Not ba-a-a-ad.
VENTRILOQUIST. We sounded pretty good, too. Too bad Rosarita's head wasn't here.
ROSARITA REFRIED *(headless body speaking)*. I was singing.
SUGAR SKULL. All right, your turn.
ALICIA. Me? I don't know any songs from Linda Ronstadt's **album.**

AZTEC PRIEST. You better remember something so we can eat.

RAMON. Think of anything. They want a few bars. He just got carried away.

ALICIA. I can't. Not even a few bars.

RAMON. Didn't you listen to any Spanish radio? Think of something you learned in school. Or heard in a movie.

ALICIA. I can't remember. I can't.

RAMON. Think. Think. You can do it.

FLAMENCO DANCER. I'm waiting.

RAMON. She'll rip your head off if you don't remember anything.

GOAT HEAD. Ain't that the truth.

RAMON. Try, Alicia. Try.

ALICIA. Okay. Okay. How about a simple song?

FLAMENCO DANCER. Anything.

ALICIA. Wait a minute. I think I remember something. All right. Here goes. *(Tries to sing.)*
    Esta son la mañanita *(Pause.)* Mañanita *(Pause.)*
    Que, que canta a... *(Hum.)* ... David
    (Rush.) Y a las pajaritos que canta
    Los cantamos a ti. *(Notices they want more.)*
    ... Spierta, me vita spierta
    La luna... *(Hum.)* ... se metio?/ Y a las muchachas, bonitas...
(Forgetting what's next.) Ah, ah.

RAMON. Is that enough?

ALL. No.

RAMON. Come on.

ALICIA. Ah, ah.

RAMON. Come, on!

ALICIA. Ah, um. Ah.

RAMON. Do it, Alicia.

Act II (or I Can't Eat Goat Head) Page 55

ALICIA. *Te lo cantamos a ti.*
SUGAR SKULL. She changed some of the words.
AZTEC PRIEST. It was out of tune.
RAMON. She sang. She sang. You didn't say she had to sing it right.
ALICIA. I wish I sang it right.
RAMON. You will pay attention to the words next time.
ALL. Let's eat!
VENTRILOQUIST. She did better than me on my first try.
ALL. Let's eat.
GOAT HEAD. Another song before we eat.
ALICIA. Listen, everyone. Thank you for everything. I'm not very hungry. Each minute that goes by, I feel like all will be lost. We have to find the pottery maker before it's too late. Before it becomes too difficult to do. I can't help this feeling inside me. I've always had it, but never understood it. I don't understand it now, but I know I have to keep looking. Don't you understand? I broke a Mexican pot.
VENTRILOQUIST *(crying)*. Maybe we should tell her where the pottery maker is.
FLAMENCO DANCER. We'll give her some clues.
AZTEC PRIEST. What a great idea.
ALICIA. Clues? Just tell me where to find him.
AZTEC PRIEST. I'll start.
SUGAR SKULL. No, I will. Door the out go just.
ALICIA. What?
FLAMENCO DANCER. There get you'll and going keep then.
ALICIA. I don't understand.
GOAT HEAD. Tunnel a see you'll.
AZTEC PRIEST. *Amigos,* right that's.
ALICIA. Oh. They're speaking backwards. A tunnel. Where?
AZTEC PRIEST. Here from far not.

ALICIA. Not-far-from-here.
AZTEC PRIEST. Right-that's.
ALICIA. Ramon! We have to find a tunnel.
RAMON. Where is it?
VENTRILOQUIST. Door the outside it see you. Here from far not.
ALICIA. I got it. Thank you. I mean, you thank.
RAMON *(confused)*. Me no speak English. *(They run out the door. The dinner guests start eating* menudo *as if nothing unusual happened. Blackout on the FLAMENCO DANCER fanning herself excessively while eating.)*

SCENE TWO

AT RISE: *Lights up on ALICIA and RAMON.*

ALICIA. There's the tunnel.
RAMON. *Aye, Chihuahua.* It's too narrow.

(They see a glass of liquid with a bilingual sign near it. It reads: DRINK ME/TOMAME. *ALICIA drinks it and she becomes thinner. They crawl through the tunnel. As they reach the end, they fall into a room of mattresses. They start to jump on them for the sheer fun of it when suddenly, feathers start to fly around. They laugh until they hear the clucking of chickens. A chicken walks by them. Then another chicken about the size of ALICIA. Then a huge chicken walks past them. He is so large, only his legs can be seen as he goes by. A MEXICAN MAN enters trying to capture the chickens.)*

Act II (or I Can't Eat Goat Head) Page 57

MEXICAN MAN. Here kitty, kitty, kitty. Here kitty, kitty, kitty. *(He sees RAMON and ALICIA.)* Were you jumping on my mattresses?

ALICIA. I'm so sorry.

MEXICAN MAN. No wonder the chickens got out. The mattresses are filled with chickens.

ALICIA and RAMON. CHICKENS?

MEXICAN MAN. Of course. Didn't you see them? Don't matter. I got chickens of all sizes. One this size, *(Demonstrates from small to big.)* one this size, and this size, and this size, and this size, and this size. Chickens of all sizes. No two are the same size. My brother uses them for the mattresses he makes. He is a mattress maker. Done it almost all his life. He doesn't get paid much for it, but it's a job that feeds his family. If he was paid more, he'd build a nice house for his family.

RAMON. Where does he live now?

MEXICAN MAN. In a shack.

ALICIA. Oh, gross. How sad!

MEXICAN MAN. But he is proud of it. Here kitty, kitty, kitty. Well, when the chickens are hungry, they'll come back. Are you looking for my brother? He went shopping. He'll be back in a little while. Come over here and let me show you around. Where did you come from?

ALICIA. I came from very far away.

MEXICAN MAN. Don't we all. You like jumping on the mattresses?

ALICIA. Yeah.

MEXICAN MAN. Go ahead and jump again.

ALICIA. Really?

MEXICAN MAN. Sure. How about him?

RAMON. Sorry, *señor*. I think we let the chickens out when we do.

MEXICAN MAN. Don't worry, I like chasing them. Here comes one now.

(The chickens enter and the three start chasing them all around. Then ALICIA chases a chicken into another room. She sees many types of beautiful pottery and in the center of it all is a pottery wheel.)

ALICIA. The pottery maker!
MEXICAN MAN and RAMON. *¿Que?*
ALICIA. We found the pottery maker!
MEXICAN MAN and RAMON. *¿Donde?*
ALICIA. He's somewhere here!
MEXICAN MAN. Oh, you found my favorite room.
ALICIA. Where is he?
MEXICAN MAN. Who?
ALICIA. *Señor* pottery maker.
MEXICAN MAN. How do you know it isn't *señora?*
ALICIA. I never thought about that. It could be *señora.*
MEXICAN MAN. That's right. But that's wrong. It's *señor* and you are looking at him.
ALICIA. The pottery maker?
RAMON. You found him, Alicia.
ALICIA. Great! But first, can you make him a new trumpet?
RAMON. Or just fix this one. I'm humble.
MEXICAN MAN *(now POTTERY MAKER).* No problem. I'm an expert. I'll make you a new one.
ALICIA. I thought you were a chicken farmer.
POTTERY MAKER. Can't one have two careers?
ALICIA. Yes, of course. Wow! We finally found you. Now I want to ask you a very important question.
POTTERY MAKER. Stay away from my pottery wheel. You break it, and it will be all over for me, and for you, too.

Act II   (or I Can't Eat Goat Head)   Page 59

RAMON. Sorry.

POTTERY MAKER. What were you going to ask? *(A small chicken runs by clucking.)* Hey, there goes my chicken! Excuse me.

RAMON. I'll get it. *(He exits.)*

POTTERY MAKER. Go on, *niña*.

ALICIA. I wanted to ask you if—

(RAMON re-enters.)

RAMON *(interrupting)*. I found it. But this chicken is small. *"Muy chica."*

POTTERY MAKER. We call her, *"Muy Chica."*

ALICIA. I'm trying to ask if—*(The pottery wheel starts to spin.)*

POTTERY MAKER. I have to hurry. I have to get to work. I have to make more pottery. *(The pottery wheel stops spinning.)* False alarm.

ALICIA. Why did the pottery wheel start, then stop spinning?

POTTERY MAKER. Whoever it was that passed away, *(Crosses himself.)* came back to life. Weren't ready. No problem. I wait. I'm very patient and so is God. *(Crosses himself, so does RAMON.)*

ALICIA. You mean, someone was going to die, and didn't?

POTTERY MAKER *(crosses himself, so does RAMON)*. Si. But it's all right. They have a good place to go when they do.

ALICIA. To heaven?

POTTERY MAKER *(crosses himself, so does RAMON)*. Si.

ALICIA. The pottery wheel spun when someone was going to—

POTTERY MAKER. —Exit. *(Crosses himself, so does RAMON.)* Their souls need a place to stay for a while. They come here to the Aztec temple and choose pottery to stay in. When they are summoned, it's their turn to go up to the gates of heaven. Hey, if that wasn't the case, the gates would be clogged up. There has to be some order.

ALICIA. But what if the pottery gets broken?

POTTERY MAKER. That's when they are summoned.

ALICIA. I don't understand.

POTTERY MAKER. When the pottery gets broken, it was meant to be. It was that soul's turn to go. Did you break some pottery recently?

ALICIA. Yes, I did. And I've been feeling guilty ever since.

POTTERY MAKER. Don't be. The soul that was in that pottery was very happy to be released. It probably knew it was his turn to go to the gates. *(Crosses himself and notices RAMON doing it, too.)* You don't have to copy me.

RAMON. I'm Catholic.

POTTERY MAKER. Oh. Let me see your trumpet. *(He gets a slab of clay and starts forming a new trumpet.)*

ALICIA. So that's where the souls go. I always wanted to know what happened to them. So breaking Mexican pottery by accident isn't a crime?

POTTERY MAKER. Of course not. We live in a world of destiny.

ALICIA. And it was that soul's destiny to be broken?

POTTERY MAKER. That's right. There you go.

RAMON. It's beautiful. Let me try it. *(He plays it.)* It's even better sounding than my old one. *Gracias, amigo.*

POTTERY MAKER. *De nada.*

ALICIA. The pottery over there have souls?

POTTERY MAKER. Not yet. They are ready to be sold at the *mercado* for soul usage.

ALICIA. Thank you, *señor* pottery maker.

POTTERY MAKER. For what?

ALICIA. For relieving my guilt.

Act II   (or I Can't Eat Goat Head)   Page 61

POTTERY MAKER. Don't worry. Things happen.

ALICIA. Yes, they do. Don't they? And when they do, you learn something from it. We have to leave now. We have to find Rosa.

POTTERY MAKER. Before you leave, let me give you something that might come in handy.

ALICIA. It's a paper flower, and a hand mirror.

POTTERY MAKER. ¡Mijia!

RAMON. You gave me enough. This new trumpet is all I need. It's my personality. *(He toots it.) Gracias por todo. (ALICIA smells the flower and then looks at the mirror.)*

ALICIA. I see Rosa! She is tied up on the Tree of Heads! The Elvira gang got her.

POTTERY MAKER. Then hurry. Here, through this ceramic door. *Adios, and buena suerte.*

(ALICIA and RAMON go through the door and are suddenly in the Village of Laughter. Mexican VILLAGERS approach laughing, and continue laughing throughout.)

RAMON. Where are we?

ALICIA. I don't know.

VILLAGER #1. You are in the Village of Laughter and today we have never laughed so hard. *(Burst of laughter from VILLAGERS.)*

VILLAGER #2. Look over there.

(They look to see ARMADILLA and HORNY TOAD surrounded by the VILLAGERS who are laughing at them hysterically.)

ALICIA. Armadilla? Horny Toad!

ARMADILLA. There you are.

HORNY TOAD. We took a wrong turn and ended up here. *(VILLAGERS burst into laughter.)*

ALICIA. Why are they laughing at you? *(Burst of laughter from VILLAGERS.)*

ARMADILLA. They've been doing it for hours.

HORNY TOAD. We told them how we were looking for you, and how depressing our lives were. Then they started laughing. *(Burst of laughter from VILLAGERS.)*

VILLAGER #3. Wouldn't you laugh, too?

ARMADILLA. No. Our lives are so sad. For generations, our families have had cause to be so sad. *(Burst of laughter from VILLAGERS.)* Stop that.

HORNY TOAD. They won't.

ARMADILLA. I tried to tell them that being fatalistic is a cultural trait, but they won't buy it. *(Burst of laughter from VILLAGERS.)*

HORNY TOAD. The Elviras have Rosa tied to the Tree of Heads!

ARMADILLA. She wanted us to tell you that she couldn't guide you anymore.

ALICIA. Guide me to what?

HORNY TOAD. To the answers.

ALICIA. What answers?

ARMADILLA. Oh, oh. We found her too early.

ALICIA. We have to help Rosa.

ARMADILLA. Rosa said to forget about her.

ALICIA. I have to save her from the Elviras like she saved me.

HORNY TOAD. Those Elviras are mean.

ALICIA. Come with me, Armadilla and Horny Toad. Together we can save her. *(ARMADILLA and HORNY TOAD are still.)* What's the matter?

Act II   (or I Can't Eat Goat Head)   Page 63

HORNY TOAD. We like it here. *(Burst of laughter from VILLAGERS.)*

ARMADILLA. Hush up, you heifers.

ALICIA. I thought you didn't like them laughing at your problems.

ARMADILLA. We don't. But every minute of laughter makes our problems seem like nothing. Maybe they were nothing all along. *(Burst of laughter from VILLAGERS.)*

HORNY TOAD. It seems like we've learned something very valuable here. That is, that it is better to laugh than cry about your problems. *(Burst of laughter from VILLAGERS.)*

ALICIA. Is this what you want, Armadilla?

ARMADILLA. Yes. I guess laughing is better. I'm waiting for it to get to me. It might take a while since I've inherited this gloomy exterior. But I think it'll come. If I sit here for a few more hours, hearing the laughter, maybe it'll start melting my problems away. Horny Toad laughed a few times.

ALICIA. You did?

HORNY TOAD. I sure did. A brick hit me on the head and the whole village laughed. *(Burst of laughter from VILLAGERS.)* I couldn't feel sorry for myself after that. They were having so much fun with it, and I thought it was hysterical. *(Burst of laughter from VILLAGERS.)*

ALICIA. Then, we'll leave you in the Village of Laughter. I'll miss you two.

ARMADILLA. Don't miss us too much. We finally found happiness, at our own expense. *Adios muchacha.*

ALICIA. *¡Que les vaya bien!*

RAMON. *¡Viva la risa!*

VILLAGERS *(much laughter)*. *¡VIVA! (They exit during the laughter. HORNY TOAD sheds a tear as he sees ALICIA and RAMON leave. ARMADILLA notices the tear and starts laughing hysterically, and cannot stop. Blackout.)*

SCENE THREE

AT RISE: *ALICIA and RAMON arrive at the Tree of Heads. ALICIA climbs up and releases ROSA who has a gag over her mouth. The HEADS are very still. Their eyes are closed.*

ALICIA. Rosa, I'm here. I'll untie you.
RAMON. The heads look like they're in a coma.
ROSA. The Elvira gang put them to sleep with sleeping pills. They stuffed it in their mouths. The heads liked you and wanted to make a lot of noise to warn you.
RAMON. That Elvira gang is too smart. What would have happened if we had given them a college education?
ROSA. They're coming! Watch out!

(The ELVIRAS enter.)

ELVIRA #1. There she is.
ELVIRA #2. Get her.
ELVIRA #3. Get her good.
ELVIRA #4. Tear her apart.
ELVIRA #1. Don't leave a single piece of her alive.
ALL ELVIRAS *(chant).* She's a *pocha,* she's a *pocha. (Etc.)*
ALICIA. You don't scare me.
RAMON. I'm scared.
ALICIA. Leave us alone. You embarrass me.
ELVIRA #1. Now we're really going to get you.
ELVIRA #2. Get down from that tree.
RAMON. The chicken claws, Alicia!
ALICIA. I'm not afraid of you. Use your *trompeta,* Ramon.
RAMON. Oh, no! It's not the original. It's not going to work.

Act II   (or I Can't Eat Goat Head)   Page 65

ALICIA. Oh, yes, it will. Give it to me. *Magia! (She blows on the trumpet and an even more beautiful sound comes out.)*

ELVIRA #1. My mascara is melting!

ALL ELVIRAS. We're melting.

ELVIRA #2. Listen to me, Elvees. PLUG YOUR EARS.

RAMON. OH, NO. They're just too, too smart. They are plugging their ears. What do we do now?

ALICIA. All I have left is this paper flower.

RAMON. Throw it! They hate cultural items.

ALICIA and RAMON. *Magia! (ALICIA throws the paper flower and it explodes into a fog. The ELVIRAS disappear. A puddle of mascara remains. ALICIA, ROSA and RAMON flee.)*

RAMON. Through the forest of mangos. Now through the *piñata* land. Now through the tortilla garden. Through the church. *(He crosses himself.)*

ALICIA. Do you know where you are going?

RAMON. Ah, sure.

ROSA. Here, through the pinto bean farm. And now through the maize. Now through the coffee bean farm.

RAMON. Is that Juan Valdez?

ROSA. Now through the Spanish Echo Tunnel.

ECHO #1, ECHO 2#, ECHO 3# *(repeat like an echo after each word)*. *Español. (Echo.) Español. (Echo.) Español. (Echo.) Corran. (Echo.) Corran. (Echo.) Corran. (Echo.)*

ALICIA. I understand that. I understand that.

RAMON and ROSA. Good. *(They run back to the Mexican curio store.)*

RAMON. We outran them.

ROSA. We are safe.

RAMON. We are safe.

ALICIA. We are, aren't we? Now I need to ask you something, Rosa. Why were you running away?

ROSA. So you can run into yourself. Do you remember your journey?

ALICIA. Yes.

ROSA. Do you remember everything you saw?

ALICIA. Yes.

ROSA. Everything?

ALICIA. I found the pottery maker.

ROSA. What else did you find?

ALICIA. I don't understand.

ROSA. Just think for a moment, and show me what you have learned. *(ALICIA thinks for a moment, RAMON blows his trumpet. ALICIA smiles and goes to a stack of Mexican blankets and brings them over. She gives one to RAMON.)*

ALICIA. See these Mexican blankets. This is what it all means. *(She gets another blanket and gives it to ROSA. She places the blankets in different spots on the floor.)* Diana, Jose, Rosario, Felipe, Patty, my mother, my father, *mis abuelos,* one for Armadilla, one for Horny Toad, and the rest are for everyone else.

RAMON. What are you doing?

ALICIA. See how no two Mexican blankets are the same? That's everyone. We are all like Mexican blankets. See how each line, and the colors, makes each blanket different? It's like us. Me, you, everyone. We are all of the same cloth. Never deny it. Never run away. See it. Know it. Be it. Accept it. *(ROSA picks one of the blankets and presents it to ALICIA.)*

ROSA. Beautiful on top, and underneath...I am glad you chose the Mexican blanket to explain who you are. You are ready to go back.

ALICIA. What? Go back home? I feel so comfortable here.

ROSA. You are ready.

RAMON. You know who you are.

Act II   (or I Can't Eat Goat Head)   Page 67

ALICIA. I always knew, but I never really wanted to acknowledge it.

RAMON *(toots his horn, then:).* Good-bye, Alicia. Always remember me. If you ever see a Mexican puppet hanging in a store, would you say, "That's a wonderful puppet." And say it real loud so someone in the shop will buy it.

ALICIA. I'll miss you, Ramon, and everything here.

RAMON. *Soy el musico tocando la trompeta. (He toots his horn again.)*

ALICIA. *Adios a todos. A todos los quiero mucho. (ROSA puts the blanket over ALICIA's head to cover her. Suddenly the blanket falls to the ground, ALICIA has disappeared. Blackout.)*

SCENE FOUR

MOM. Alicia. Alicia.

AT RISE: *Lights come up on ALICIA opening her eyes. She is in a wicker chair at the curio shop. A Mexican blanket is on her lap. The shopkeeper turns off his Spanish radio station which has just finished playing a ranchera. ALICIA awakens fully, she sees her MOTHER and the STOREKEEPER smiling at her.*

STOREKEEPER. *Ya vez.* I told you she would be fine.
ALICIA. Ramon!
STOREKEEPER. Ramon? *Me llamo Don Ricardo.*
ALICIA. Do you play a trumpet?
STOREKEEPER. When I was fourteen.

MOM. Alicia. You hit your head very hard. I thought for a moment I lost you.

ALICIA. *I* was lost, but then I found my way.

MOM. *Se pego, pero bien pegada.*

ALICIA. I went everywhere.

MOM. Where did you go?

ALICIA. I went with Ramon to find the Aztec temple. I didn't know where to find the pottery maker. He was supposed to tell me where the souls from the pottery would go after the pottery broke.

MOM. *Mija,* you broke Mexican pottery. Over there where the pieces are. That's where you tripped.

ALICIA. But I got up right away to see where you were going.

MOM. Me?

ALICIA. This doll. *Un muñeca. (Looks at MOM, then focuses on the STOREKEEPER.)* And you had strings. *Y mirer un* armadillo *y un* horny toad. They were looking for me. Everyone was looking for each other. Oh, but the Elvira gang was scary. *Tenian* chicken claws. *Las caras como Elvira,* the empress of night, on TV. *Y conoci la* Tree of Heads *y comi menudo* with the Aztec priest's guests. Oh, the goat head wanted me to eat his *ojos.* There was the maze of velvet paintings, and—

MOM *(interrupting). Niña, estabas soñiando.* And she's speaking some Spanish. Not too good, but okay.

ALICIA. *Era todo cierto.*

MOM. Hear that? *¡Español!* Honey. He picked you up and brought you to this chair. You were smiling so we just watched you.

ALICIA. I was smiling?

STOREKEEPER. You woke up soon after.

Act II (or I Can't Eat Goat Head) Page 69

ALICIA. Wait a minute. We jumped on mattresses made of chickens.

STOREKEEPER. Now take her to a doctor. *(ALICIA gets up and goes to the shelf. She sees a stuffed armadillo and a horny toad.)*

ALICIA. It's Armadilla and Horny Toad. Here's the flamenco dancer, and the Mexican villagers in the Land of Laughter.

STOREKEEPER. That's the doll shelf. I have all kinds. The doll in your hand belongs there. The armadillo is three hundred dollars.

MOM. What do we want with a stuffed armadillo when we can run over one in Tejas?

(ALICIA sees the piñatas overhead. She then walks to a puppet rack where a wide variety of puppets hang. RAMON is hanging there with a trumpet glued to his hand. ALICIA stares at ROSA, the doll on the shelf.)

MOM. It's time to go, Alicia. *(ALICIA is very sad.)* I bought this Mexican blanket for my friend. You think she'll like it? *(Pause.)* I'll buy that Mexican doll. It's not a toy. For decoration. Put it on your vanity table.

STOREKEEPER. That's good. She has fingerprints all over it.

MOM. *Y tambien el titere.*

STOREKEEPER. This is my lucky day. *Un musico tocando la trompeta.* I'll add this in for no extra charge. *(He puts a paper flower in the bag.)*

ALICIA. A paper flower. Thank you.

STOREKEEPER. And don't go falling on pottery again.

ALICIA. Did we pay for the broken pottery?

STOREKEEPER. It's all right. It was time for it to get broken.

ALICIA. Why? Why?

STOREKEEPER. It was just time.

MOM. Alicia, let's go. *(ALICIA won't move.)* Alicia. *Aye. Vamanos.* All right. Here, Alicia. *(MOM takes a sugar skull out of her shopping bag.)* I was going to give this to you later, and tell you how important it was in—

ALICIA. The Day of the Dead sugar skull.

STOREKEEPER *(surprised)*. *Mirala.* She knows what it's for.

MOM. Well, it was worth coming here. I didn't even know what this was for when I was growing up. We never used this up north. This is *"puro centro Mexico."* Come on now. *(Hesitation from ALICIA.)* Don't tell me you have energy to go to the mall. *(ALICIA shakes her head no.)* Good. I'm hungry. How about you?

ALICIA. *Un poco.* What's for dinner?

MOM. Your dad is going to cook *cabeza de chivo.*

ALICIA. GOAT HEAD?

MOM. It's a special occasion.

ALICIA. I can't eat goat head.

MOM. Well, you don't have to. I have *menudo* in the refrigerator. *Vamanos, por que se va el tren. (She exits.)*

STOREKEEPER. *Adios, niña.*

MOM *(off)*. Alicia! *(ALICIA turns towards the STOREKEEPER. He urges her to go, but she is hesitating.)*

STOREKEEPER *(with a wink of his eye)*. Pronto, pronto. *(STOREKEEPER said "pronto, pronto" exactly the way RAMON did in SCENE TWO. ALICIA turns in surprise, then is extremely happy over her whole experience.)*

ALICIA *(exits, singing)*. *Y andale.*

END OF PLAY

DIRECTOR'S NOTES

DIRECTOR'S NOTES